BUILDING A VISION BOARD

Tess Denton

Printed in the United States of America

First Printing, 2012
ISBN-13: 978-1475103182
ISBN-10: 1475103182

Destiny Rising, LLC

www.tessdenton.com

Contents

Introduction

People are fascinating. We are driven by our emotions and beliefs. Each of us employs a unique logic to life that we have spent our lifetime creating. We make hundreds of decisions every day based on this unique logic. Our decisions, both major and minor, affect how grand or limited a life we imagine and create for ourselves. The life we believe we deserve is often the life we create.

I have always believed that people deserve to be happy. By age 7, I had theorized that when people laugh, they feel better - if even for a moment. From that point forward, I became interested in helping people feel free to imagine, and to enjoy life. I wanted to create and provide people with joyful and humorous moments so that they could feel better more often.

I thought that if a person could step away from the problems in their life for even a few minutes, they would reset their well-being meter. I figured that if the mind and body took a recess from stress, one could handle the next challenge that life set before them.

As a young adult, my chosen method of helping others step away from their stress was humor. I spent a number of years studying improvisational comedy at Players Workshop and The Second City Training Center in Chicago and working in comedy groups. Over time, life led me to other cities and other professions. I still maintain a passion for helping people find humor and peace and connect with work and play that makes them happy most often. In fact, helping people connect with work and play that makes them happy is a key reason why I wrote this book.

When I remember to reconnect with the young and fresh version of myself, I regain my sense of excitement and possibility. Truth be known, being overly serious about business limits my potential. I feel most alive and my life works best when I infuse my work with lots of play and creativity. It is no wonder that I love my work in the area of Vision Boards and vision processes. When I offer Vision Board Workshops to individuals and teams, I have the opportunity to combine my creative and business experience and have fun doing it.

When I was young, my source of creativity and imagination was close to home. I grew up outside of Chicago in the 1960's and 1970's, in a white frame house built sometime around 1940. At the end of our driveway was my laboratory for creativity and imagination. The laboratory was actually a freestanding one car white wooden garage with no door. The garage was so packed with bicycles, sleds, bases, balls, and bats that no car could fit in it. In this setting, all manner of make-believe occurred.

Rarely was the garage simply a garage. The garage was often a farmhouse, a school, a dime store, an office, a theater, a grocery store, a doctor's office, a hospital, an airport, and a train station. For our family and the kids in the neighborhood, our garage really was all of these things. In my mind, I really was a doctor, a principal, a checker, a farmer, a mother, a patient, an actor, a flight attendant, etc. Having a place to imagine what the future might hold and to set dreams in motion was a gift. Today, an important source of my creativity and imagination is Vision Boards.

I hope that *Building A Powerful Vision Board* offers you a place to imagine and serves as a source of inspiration to create a life you love. As you read *Building A Powerful Vision Board*, complete the activities, and build a variety of Vision Boards, your ability to connect with your belief in what is possible for your life will increase.

My goal in writing *Building A Powerful Vision Board* is that the content and exercises help you create your vision for a bold and bright future. I want you to feel as if you have an all-day pass that allows you to be, to do and have anything you want.

Part One
On Vision Boards

Chapter One

*Set The Stage For a **Bolder** Picture of Your Life*

If you were to write the story of your life up to this point, would it be the story you want to tell?

Are you happy with how your life is turning out?

Is life charging you up or depleting your energy?

If you are not being energized by your life, who or what is draining your energy and controlling your destiny?

Being in control of what is happening in your life means different things at different life stages. Responsibilities that take control may include parenthood, eldercare, or providing for your family. Employment downsizing, health issues, and finance are also factors that either add to your passion or drain you of time to focus on your dreams and aspirations.

At some life stages, your responsibilities can require 100% of your attention, leaving you void of "me" time. During such times, it is all you can do to get through the day or the workweek in order to get some sleep and prepare for the week ahead. I have traveled in those shoes and respect the "giving" years. Critical commitments are valid and need to be honored.

Ideally, there comes a moment when you can reclaim your life, your dreams and your goals. When you do pick them up again, they may be out of date and out of sync with who you have become and what you want in life.

Welcome to your new journey. You may have found that you can attend to your own passions and dreams 1% or 5% or 10% of the time, and you want to seize this opportunity to make the most of your life. *Building A Powerful Vision Board* will help you find your most passionate connection with work, play, and life. I had an Improvisational instructor who first told me, "The life you're living isn't a dress rehearsal". With this thought in mind, today is a perfect day for you to create the path that leads you to a life you love.

Building A Powerful Vision Board has been designed to help you create that path. The book is divided into three segments: Part One defines and explains Vision Boards, how to create them and the benefits of using a Vision Board process to achieve your goals and what you want in life. Part Two is activity focused. It includes eight Vision Board projects. Each Vision Board project includes a ninety-day Destined for Success roadmap to achieving your vision. Part Three contains recommendations for your journey, a resource guide, and additional vision activities.

Chapter Two

Vision Boards – What They Are and How They Are Created

What Is A Vision Board?

A Vision Board is a method of goal setting and life transformation. It is a visual expression of what you would like to see present in your life. The process of creating a Vision Board provides an opportunity to spend focused time and energy reflecting on specific items, elements, and situations you want to attract into your present and future. Creating a Vision Board is a chance for you to be selfish. In fact, it is a requirement!

You do not have to validate why you are deserving of anything you place on your Vision Board. There are no calories or carbohydrates to count. You can indulge all you want. There are no deadlines or cost analyses or budgets to submit. Nothing you ask for is too small or too large, too much or too little. The board is not about what you want to exclude from your life. Rather, it is all about inclusion. There is no right or wrong or grade assigned.

You might ask yourself, "Once I have created my Vision Board, what's going to happen? What are my next steps?" These are excellent questions. Investing time on the deliberate activity of focusing thought and intention, and being non-resistant to your ideas, hopes and aspirations is probably something you do not often do. Usually, you have an idea, that idea creates a positive impulse and you hold the idea about "wouldn't it be nice if…" for a short time. Then, you quickly cancel out the positive influence by noting why it is not possible or plausible for you to be, to do or have what you want.

To counteract this discounting tendency, the Vision Board creation processes I have created will help you maintain your attention to your intention. Your Vision Board will keep you from discounting your ideas. Your Vision Board is your tool for bringing your attention back to what it is you desire, each time you look at it.

How Do I Make A Vision Board?

Making a Vision Board is far more than a cut and paste activity. Creating a Vision Board that will help you forge a path to a meaningful, successful, and transformed life is a multi-phased process. Assembling a Vision Board is the final step in the process. You need more than poster board, scissors, glue sticks and some pictures to build a better life.

Prior to construction and assembly of your Vision Board, you need to build a compelling and colorful story of what you want for yourself. You also need to create a clear picture in your mind of how you want your life to unfold. Your Vision Board is your outward facing version of the vision you hold in your mind. Creating A *Powerful Vision Board* is filled with tools that will help you clarify your goals, clear up confusion about your priorities and prepare you for making bold life changes and setting a path to prosperity.

For each Vision Board you create using the *Building A Powerful Vision Board* processes as your guide, you will build a clear and descriptive picture in your mind, in your heart and on paper. You will also have a ninety-day plan to move toward your vision.

11

Each time you create a Vision Board you will want to display it in a place of prominence. Place it in a space you enjoy, where it can serve as a positive reminder of what your life will include – more money, travel, a fit and fantastic you, a new job, your dream home, a new car, or time with your grandchildren. Many people choose to display their Vision Boards in their kitchen, bedroom, or office.

Chapter Three

Getting Clear on Your Vision For Your Future

Vision is often referred to as a *dream*, thought, concept, or object formed by the imagination and a manifestation to the senses of something immaterial. Vision has been the topic of many highly acclaimed books. Napoleon Hill's *Think & Grow Rich*, Esther and Jerry Hicks' *Ask and It is Given* and Shakti Gawain's *Creative Visualization* are among the most well known books on the topic.

I have designed *Building A Powerful Vision Board* as a manual you can use to assess your priorities, construct effective Vision Boards, and create a roadmap to achieving your vision. *Building A Powerful Vision Board* will enable you to create your vision for a strong and bright future that resonates with what is most important in your life, work, and play. *Building A Powerful Vision Board* is not intended as a one-time read. It provides what you need to take a fresh look at your goals and aspirations with different Vision Boards over time. You can work on your own, or use the book with a spouse or friends or even at work.

As you begin to think about the focus of your vision for your life, consider the following: Your plans, your dreams, and your goals in the areas of relationships, finance, career, and lifestyle. Your vision begins with a picture in your mind. Often, pictures in our minds happen without conscious awareness. As you read this paragraph, images are being created in your mind as you register the words with no effort. There is no predicting what images your mind may produce, and these images are generally fleeting. You may see images of a stairway cluttered with laundry that needs to be taken to the second floor and put away, or, you may picture a European café where you would like to dine on your honeymoon, or you may experience an image of you being selected as a principal or partner in your firm.

I have discovered that my mind's picture stimulates a thought; the thought creates an idea, that idea creates an *Aha!* moment and the process of asking for what I want begins. As you work with the exercises in *Building A Powerful Vision Board*, you will use the ideas, hopes, and aspirations about your career, your life, and your possessions to make an expressive and bold external rendition of them. Your Vision Boards will help you maintain your focus on the life you are intending to create.

If you have ever been asked to "hold that thought" while someone steps away to take a call or answer the door, you know that it takes effort to remember what you were just thinking and feeling. Thoughts are fleeting but your Vision Board is not. It empowers you to return time and again to the picture of what you want to attract into your life. Remember that thoughts become things. Energy begets more energy, and your vision can become your reality. Know that your life and your journey are about to take on greater clarity.

Chapter Four

Why Now Is The Perfect Time to Create a Vision Board

Many people are recovering from a hope deficit. In 2009, when I started writing *Building A Powerful Vision Board*, a deficit of possibility existed in the United States. The economy had plummeted. A depressed economy creates a decrease in consumer confidence about personal earning capacity, a decrease in their willingness to taking risks and a lack of confidence about one's future being bright. Scores of people with new business ideas or plans to fund retirement through entrepreneurial ventures retreated from making the entrepreneurial leap to work they loved. Instead, people began living on a steady diet of "getting by". The economy has still not fully recovered, and the financial tension was and still is palpable.

When you live with a "getting by" mentality for long enough, and your thoughts about your future extend only to "I'm just lucky I've got a job", your candle begins to dim. Sadness and resignation result in fear and discouragement.

Building A Powerful Vision Board is a tonic for fear and discouragement. It offers a perfect opportunity to get clear about what it is that will make you happy, as well as identifying and eliminating negative thought and response patterns. Working with this book provides a space and opportunity to list, visualize, prioritize, and declare your intentions.

It is only when we are clear about what we want that we can move in a direction to fulfill our dreams. Cheshire Cat from Lewis Carrol's, *Alice in Wonderland*, is attributed with the following quote: "If you don't know where you're going, then any road will do." The power in *Building A Powerful Vision Board* is that you begin your journey to somewhere specific in your life - a journey to wealth, a journey to a remarkable marriage, a journey to owning your own company. Your Vision Board is not a turn-by-turn navigator. The Vision Board process helps you find your inspiration as you determine your destination. Your Vision Board heralds your destination.

Chapter Five

5 Key Benefits of Creating a Vision Board

You may be seeking to build a multimillion-dollar business, to meet the love of your life or to build your dream home. Vision Boards are instruments that support your journey to living a fulfilling and effective life. *Building A Powerful Vision Board* will help you achieve appreciation of the abundance currently in your life. You will reawaken your dreams and ambition, develop a keen awareness of what is important to you and progress toward your goals.

The exercises in this book are ideal to use in working on your own or with a small group of people. Work teams will find the exercises a good way to increase their understanding of others' priorities, creative styles, and goals.

I have identified 5 key benefits you will achieve from reading and doing the work in *Building A Powerful Board*: Clarity, Hope, Confidence, Momentum, and Happiness.

Clarity is energizing. It is refreshing to clear away doubt about the direction you are headed, as well as what you do and do not want in your life.

Hope fuels your fire. Hope is the emotional state that promotes your belief in a positive outcome. Even saying "Hope" offers relief and a sense of possibility. In a world where doors close and we become discouraged, the Hope that a Vision Board provides is a powerful tool to combat discouragement and doubt.

Confidence results from creating a realistic and well developed plan. Once you have clarified what it is you want in your life, you can begin forging a path toward your goals.

Momentum increases once your vision is established, your goals are identified, and your plan is in action. Without a vision for what you want in life, you will likely be limited to motion or small movement in no particular direction.

Happiness is the result of the four benefits listed above. You are clear about what you want, you are hopeful that you can fulfill your dreams, you are confident that you will reach your destination, and your momentum will swiftly take you there. Happiness also results from enjoying the journey, not just the arrival at your destination.

Chapter Six

How Vision Boards Yield Results

I have been practicing creative visualization and studying the Law of Attraction for more than twenty years. I believe that thoughts become things and that we are powerful attractors of situations and results in our lives. I live a life of constant coincidence. I have learned to be careful about what I ask for, because I am very good at attracting what I ask for into my life.

You will soon find that the thought and intention you invest in a Vision Board are as important as creating the physical board itself. The intention setting that you do in advance of the physical creation of a Vision Board is often the most powerful component of the board. You may be surprised at how quickly you will begin noticing that what you intend shows up in your life.

As you begin watching for results from your Vision Board, keep in mind that initial signs of attracting what you have asked for are subtle. I hold loosely and optimistically to the expectation that my Vision Board will yield results identical to the images I place on the board. As for the timeline of things showing up, I am careful not to ask, "Are we there yet? Are we there yet? Are we there yet?" I take great care at the front end of the process to be clear about my intentions. I have learned to trust that things happen in their right time.

For me, a benefit of creating a Vision Board that goes beyond the benefits mentioned in Chapter Five is an ever-increasing understanding of my key priorities and of myself. I am constantly evolving, just as you are. What held glamour and promise to me five or ten years ago is very different than it is today. Your life begins to shift when you set new priorities. These shifts can be rewarding. The shifts can also be challenging and conflict producing, particularly if you are more prepared for changes than are the people around you. When you encounter resistance, be patient with yourself and others. Remember to keep your focus on the vision you have created and the resulting benefits of achieving what you want in life.

When I am clear about my path and know where I am headed, I am happy. If I become bogged down and attend to others' priorities before my own, I can lose sight of my path. One way that I focus on my own priorities is by taking advantage of cancelled appointments, twenty-minute waits for a train or a friend's arrival at a restaurant. I have a deck of vision cards (each has an intention on it). I review these and make notes about how the intention is showing up in my life. Stealing times such as these each month is a delicious luxury that costs nothing and helps me stay connected with my priorities.

When I revisit a Vision Board, I am often surprised that small intentions placed on it have manifested. I have started a BlogTalk Radio program titled: "Shop Talk". While reviewing a Vision Board from two years ago, I noticed that the BlogTalk Radio icon was adjacent to the term "Shop Talk". When I titled the program, I had no recollection of having placed those words on my board.

Begin taking note of coincidence and serendipity at play in your life. Focus on listening in the first few weeks after you create a Vision Board. Tune in to conversations on the bus or on a plane, at restaurants, and at work. You will likely find that people who have the same priorities and interests as you start showing up in your life. It may suddenly seem as if everyone is talking about the same things you are! I have heard it said that if you decide to purchase a certain car, you begin seeing that car all around you. You may be seeing more of them or you may just be attuned to noticing them. Whichever the case, your senses are heightened.

Your new priorities will begin to influence your day-to-day life. You will take the desires you have listed on your Vision Board into consideration when making decisions about relationships, finances, or personal and professional commitments. It is natural, it is normal, and it is another indication that your Vision Board is creating results.

Chapter Seven

Preparing to Create Your Vision Board

Creating a truly powerful Vision Board is a process with a beginning, middle, and an end. The magic occurs as much in the early stages of imagination and clarification as it does in assembling and displaying your Vision Board. As you will recall from Chapter Two, assembling your Vision Board is the final step in the process of creating a Vision Board.

You could ignore my advice, and jump right to assembling a Vision Board. People often do simply clip, place and paste photos on a board without any preparation and process work. Resist the urge of choosing to jump ahead in creating a Vision Board without clarification, directional inspiration, or goals in mind. If you jump ahead, I believe you will miss an important leg of the journey.

If you like to get right down to business, or are a results driven individual, it may take discipline and self-control for you to engage in the essential pre-work of the Vision Board process. The discipline will be worth the effort. If you are an artist, a cook, or a crafter, you are probably comfortable with the preparation and the process involved in creating a work of art.

There is no best way to build a Vision Board. I do not believe that there are hard and fast rules about how a Vision Board should be constructed. However, I will share what works best for me. The process I follow is one that supports being "in the zone", and I follow my intuition. If you study Feng Shui or if you are an avid scrap-booker, you may have an established method or preference for the placement of pictures, phrases, and textures on your board.

When I get ready to create a Vision Board, I turn on the stereo and let myself daydream while I select and clip photos and phrases. Next, I spread everything out on a table in front of me. The items that jump out at me are the first to make their way to the board. I like to use phrases to frame my photos, and I prefer to leave no empty spaces on my board. Some people like to have more blank space and simplicity. This is a personal choice.

I often group pictures on my Vision Board by topic. For example, as I neared the end of writing this book, I created a Vision Board to help motivate me as I moved through the final phase of my project. This board focuses on what great things may result from publishing my book. For the past twenty years, nearly everyone I know who wants to get their message out to the masses has said, "If I could be featured on *The Oprah Show*, then I would be really successful". Well, I did not make it to *The Oprah Show* during its run. However, like tens of thousands of others, I share the desire to be on a leading talk show. This desire has bubbled to the surface for me on dozens of occasions.

I placed photos of leading daytime talk show hosts beside a picture of me. We are smiling and facing one another. I am included in the group of women who are informing millions of people on a daily basis. Being a part of this group of women will take the message I want to share with the world to a new level. Furthermore, leading daytime talk show hosts are not struggling to get their message heard. People tune in to hear what they think and what they recommend. I would like that to happen in my life! Including these thoughts and aspirations on my Vision Board was very important to me. I know well that thoughts are things and that if you want to take your game to a new level, it is wise to surround yourself with people who are already doing what you would like to do. Therefore, I am envisioning these women as my colleagues.

In terms of beauty: I have noticed that over time, the Vision Boards I create have become more artful than they were when I first started creating

24

them. Perhaps this is because I now frame them and hang them in my office. Colors and words that "pop" are meaningful to me. Color plays a much larger role in my boards today than it did five years ago. I do not worry about my Vision Boards being attractive to others. What is important is that I connect with the messages and ideas conveyed on them.

I do not create Vision Boards with a linear storyline or a timeframe, and I do not try to create boards so that they make sense to other people. Each Vision Board holds a message and vibration for me. Life has a timeline of its own, and the Universe is wise. When I try to impose insistence and limits on my desires, I limit results. Therefore, I try to quiet the voice in me that loves to live by a clock and calendar.

When I have completed a Vision Board, I often have a pile of leftover pictures and phrases. I put these leftovers into a box and I save them for later use. Each photo and phrase I have selected resonated with me on some level, or I would not have taken the time to choose it. I open my box of extras each time I start a new Vision Board and sort through it to see if its contents might hold a place on my new Vision Board. Some phrases or photos that once held appeal no longer have a place in my heart, my desires, or my mind. I have witnessed my own evolution through many years of creating Vision Boards.

Now that you have a thorough understanding of what is involved in creating a Vision Board, you are ready to move on to the process of creating your Vision Boards. In order to complete the exercises and Vision Board projects you will find in Part Two, you will want to gather and purchase the items listed below.

Poster Board (the kind you might use for a science project) or Foam Board (I prefer this because it is sturdy)

Index Cards

A set of Colored Markers (thin)

Glue Sticks

Scissors

Ruler

Magazines, Catalogues

Chapter Activity Worksheets, Roadmaps, Powerful Word Packs
www.buildingapowerfulvisionboard.com/forms
Password: **possibilities**

Picture Frames (I love to shop garage sales and buy art for the frames. Often, wires and hangers are already in place. Disassemble the frame and measure your blank poster board against the existing art piece [or flip it over and use it for your board])

Textile Items (fabrics, flowers, trinkets)

Music (inspiring, calming, energizing)

Blank Notebook (Spiral Bound or Hardcover is ideal)

Camera

Part Two
Building Vision Boards: Exercises, Activities, and Processes

Chapter Eight

Assessing The Present And Accessing The Future

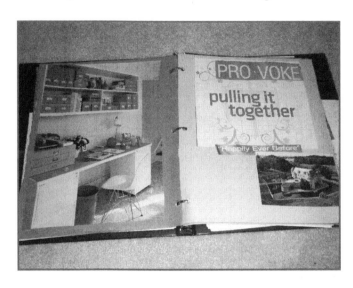

This chapter consists of four exercises that will help you gain an understanding of where you stand today in relation to your desires and beliefs about deserving success and reaching your goals. Your life today is different than it was five years ago, and it will be different five years from now. The good fortune or misfortunes you have experienced influence your perspective about success and possibility in your future.

After completing the exercises, you will be equipped with greater self-awareness in these areas as you move on to the Vision Board activities and processes. Enjoy your journey!

Where You Stand In Relation To Your Future

Exercise One
Establish Your Baseline of Optimism and Belief

As it relates to Vision Boards, your baseline is the point from which you will begin moving in the direction of your vision for your future. On a scale of 1-10, 10 being high, **what is your baseline of belief that you can and will achieve the future you desire?**

Determine your baseline of belief calculation on the continuum below:

The number you select is neither good nor bad. It is neither right nor wrong. Your number simply provides you with a sense of certainty in this moment, that you can dramatically change your life for the better.

If you selected a number that is 8 or higher, you are most likely an optimist. It is probably easy for you to imagine everything you wish for in life coming to you. You will really enjoy building your Vision Board. In fact, you may create two or three Vision Boards in the next month!

If you selected the number 4 or lower you may have a critical inner voice that serves you with negative messages. If you find yourself using limiting phrases such as "Yeah, but", "That's great, except that", and "It'll never happen" when you embark on new projects, it is not a surprise that your baseline is not on the high side. If you find it difficult to maintain a sense of optimism about your future, you may wish to seek the regular company of an uplifting group of peers.

Be aware of the mindset and language of the company you keep. It is easy to be drawn to doubt and disappointment if the people around you exude this energy. You might benefit from a daily practice of listening to uplifting belief-building speakers. In the Resource Guide at the end of the book, I have provided a list of authors, coaches, and speakers who have inspired me in the past two decades.

Remember that you are embarking on a new phase in your life. You are setting out to create a brighter vision, set a new direction, and fulfill grand goals for your life. You are unique, as are your experiences in life. Whether your self-scoring on your baseline of belief is a 2 or a 10, tapping into encouragement to nourish you on your journey to achieving your vision will positively influence your Vision Board and your staying power to turn desire into reality.

Exercise Two
Assessing Your Response To New Experiences

Life happens to some people while other people happen to life. If you are going on an adventure to create a revised future, one that matches the epic vision in your mind, you will need to forge new territories and develop tools and habits to help you stay the course. Now might be a good time to reflect on how you approach new experiences and challenging projects.

If you seriously and absolutely intend and desire to change your future, you will want to master your project completion skills so that you can stay the course on your journey. Everyone's path to achieving what they want in life meets with adversity.

As you prepare to work with Vision Boards as a tool to help you change your life, which of the following describes you?

_____ Regardless of any hardships life presents, I carry on. I turn resistance into resilience.

_____ I am confused and do not even know how to begin selecting priorities. I know that you need to set a new direction and reprioritize, and that is all I know.

_____ I have been waiting for this time in my life. My responsibilities have shifted and now is my time to make my mark on the world. I will use my resources and experiences to build a life that pleases me.

_____ I am up for considering some changes in my life, but if I receive too much negative feedback or do not have early success, I am likely to get discouraged and retreat.

_____ I am up for all adventures. I am ready to turn my life upside down and start anew. I thrive on the excitement of major change.

Exercise Three
Look Straight Ahead

List twenty items, relationships and situations that you would like to attract into your life.

1.
2.
3.
4.
5.
6.
7.
8.
9.
10.
11.
12.
13.
14.
15.
16.
17.
18.
19.
20.

Your Vision Boards are about your preferred future, about freshness and the opportunity to begin again. Often, when talking about the future, we point to mistakes of the past or projects we had to abandon due to financing, life's commitments, or fear of risk.

While intended to safeguard against future disappointment and adversity, revisiting mistakes of the past creates thoughts of defeat. As you prepare to create your new future, be mindful of negative self-talk and criticism from others. It is essential that you surround yourself with positive and supportive people who encourage you and keep you focused on a bright future.

Exercise Four
Squeaky Clean Intentions

Take five minutes to scrub your list from the previous exercise (Look Straight Ahead) of any negative phrasing it may contain. For example, if an item on your list reads "no more dead-end client prospects", transform that statement into a positive intention. Use verbiage such as "ample client contracts with projects that pay in 30 days".

Trust the process. We are generally attracted to positive people because they have positive things to say. Positive people keep us energized and optimistic. Think of your list in the same way. The more positive you can make it, the more powerful your vision will be.

Congratulations! By completing these four exercises, you have already increased your ability to build powerful Vision Boards. You have established a baseline for your belief in achieving your vision, you have made an honest assessment of how you respond to new experiences, you have created an initial list of what you would like to attract into your life, and you have given the list more power by eliminating negative verbiage.

Enjoy your journey!

Chapter Nine

You've Got to Accentuate The Positive

When you create Vision Boards, you will typically use pictures and phrases. Selecting bold and colorful pictures to place on your board is easy. Magazines, travel guides, old calendars, and the Internet are rich resources for pictures. Creating bold and colorful phrasing may take a bit of practice. This chapter demonstrates how to develop positive and inspiring phrasing.

Phrases that create a positive feeling might include:

Reach For The Stars
See The World
Stage A Comeback
Be The Change You Want To See In The World
Be A Star
Choose Happiness
Make An Impact

Select and develop positive and directive statements for your Vision Board. Positive and directive statements will reinforce your intentions for your vision. Repetition and reinforcement create thought habits that beckon the changes you want to see in your life.

Using intentional and positive statements will help distance you from the energy draining language you encounter in the media on a daily basis. Review the statements above one more time. The statements are actually a collection of embedded commands. They command you to take action. Notice how much more powerful and energized those statements are than the following statements:

> If I could find a way out of my awful job, then I would be able to reach for the stars.

> If I had more money, I would finally have a chance to see the world.

> If I weren't so afraid that people would view me as a has-been, I'd make an effort to stage a comeback.

> I'd like to make a difference in the world, but realistically, I doubt I could make it happen.

> Once upon a time, I wanted to be a star.

> I wish I could be happy.

> What can I do to make an impact?

When you create Vision Boards, you will want to be sure to use positive, present tense statements. A good practice is to select words and phrases that complete the statement "I am..." Here are a few examples: Creative, Dynamic, Successful, Wealthy, Beyond Compare, Packed with Limitless Potential and Heading for Success.

As you work on naming things you want in your life, make certain that they are colorful and descriptive. Let your imagination run wild! It costs nothing and makes the day more interesting. The result will be a powerful Vision Board. Complete the following exercise. It will serve as a primer for creating positive, powerful statements for your Vision Boards.

34

Chapter Activity
Top Ten List

Using Exercise Three (Look Straight Ahead) from Chapter Eight, select ten of the items, relationships and situations that you would like to attract into your life and list them below.

1. _____
2. _____
3. _____
4. _____
5. _____
6. _____
7. _____
8. _____
9. _____
10. _____

Now that you have selected ten items, we will focus on adding color and punch to what you have written. Include descriptive words to make your statements more powerful. Think back to grade school English class and sentence diagrams. As you may recall, a simple sentence might read, "Jane took a trip". A more descriptive sentence might read, "Jane took an exciting plane trip to Rio for her 40th birthday". The second sentence tells a more compelling story. To me, Jane's trip sounds more interesting and colorful when descriptive words are added. I not only know that Jane took a trip, I now know where she went and how she got there.

Make Ten Ideas Come Alive

Working from the list in your vision notebook, or the activity sheets you have completed, create ten descriptive, powerful, and colorful phrases that have clarity and "sell" your desire.

1.
2.
3.
4.
5.
6.
7.
8.
9.
10.

Chapter Ten

Awaken the Dreamer Within

Sometimes, the twists and turns that life presents provide an unexpected opportunity to reinvent yourself. Connecting with your hopes and dreams does not always come in a pretty package. Relocation, downsizing, being newly single, retirement, or the event of your last child starting school or leaving school are times when you may decide to follow your bliss.

As you awaken to your reinvention, trust that you are creative and imaginative. It is human nature to wish and want. It is natural to imagine and daydream. Trust that if you have set your childhood dreams and goals aside, your creative spirit is still intact. You have probably redirected and channeled your best creative energies into the lives of those you love or into a career that has helped pay your bills.

When we are very young, most of us live in a world of wonder, discovery, and make-believe. As we move into school and take our place in society, we are encouraged to be realistic and to make sensible choices in order to be successful. I have been fortunate to maintain my connection to creativity and imagination for most of my life. As an adult, I have held fast to my participation in activities focused on imagination. Just a few years after college, I decided to pursue my goal of working in a creative field and started living the life of a young free spirit: theater and improvisation classes, auditions, shows, commercials, restaurant and temporary office work assignments. I followed those dreams for a number of years.

As I look back at the choices I made at age twenty-five, they were not as unorthodox as my parents feared they might be. To me, following my dream and staying connected with my creative source was the obvious choice, albeit financially risky. What I learned about myself, life, and the reward of living a life I loved was extraordinary.

By age thirty-five, I had settled back into a sensible and logical career path. This worked very well for me for about fifteen years. However, my independent spirit was only on hiatus. By my late forties, I had a new goal of helping others pursue and achieve their dream of living a life they love.

What does life have in store for you? Let's find out.

Chapter Activity
Reconnecting With The Past

The purpose of this activity is to reacquaint you with your creative self and to see how active your creative self is in your life. This activity requires that you leave your house. Please be sure that you have completed the exercises in Chapter Eight before you start this activity.

1. Gather the tools and materials you will need to create a Vision Board (See Chapter Seven). You will create the board after you have returned from your field trip. You will use your list of twenty items and the questions from this exercise to build the Vision Board.

2. Bring this activity sheet with you along with your "List of Twenty Items" from Exercise Three in Chapter Eight.

3. Grab a Popsicle, a glass of Kool-Aid, or other favorite childhood treat.

4. Now, it is time for your field trip. If you are still living where you spent your childhood and it is filled with pleasant memories, go back to your old neighborhood and walk the path you used to take to school, your favorite park, to ballet class or baseball practice, to Brownies or Cub Scouts or to the swimming pool. You probably dreamed about your future on this path for some or all of your childhood. If you no longer live close to home, find a neighborhood where you can reignite these memories, and go there.

If you would like to create a new memory set, find a spot where, as a child, you could let your mind be free (a children's bookstore or the children's section of your local library).

Ignite your senses. You have already got the taste sense covered with your Popsicle, Kool-Aid, or treat. Tune in to sounds and scents of the season. If you are in a familiar space, what scents have come alive again? For example, when I walk into the Thomas Ford Memorial Library in Western Springs, Illinois, there is an unmistakable scent of books. When I open the door to that stone building, I am carried back to a time when

Story Hour, Summer Book Club, and wagons full of borrowed books filled my days.

Let your mind wander while you savor your Popsicle or develop a Kool-Aid moustache. Let the cloak of adulthood slip away. Once you have ignited your senses, turn to your "List of Twenty Items", and consider it in light of your childhood dreams. Ask yourself these questions and write your answers on your activity sheet:

> Are there elements of what I had hoped for when I was young on my list? If so, which items on your list are they? If not, consider adding these elements to your list.

> Is my path in sync with the interests and passions I had when I was younger?

> If I could have anything in the world, what would I choose?

> How can I integrate those things that I hoped for when I was young into my life today to increase my happiness?

1. Once you have answered the questions above, it is time to return home to create your Vision Board. When you arrive home and are ready to build your Vision Board, review the list you revised while on your field trip. Use it as a guide for selecting pictures and phrases that illustrate your passions.

2. Post your "List of Twenty Items" and the questions you answered during this activity next to your Vision Board or paste them on the back of your Vision Board.

3. Complete the Destined for Success Roadmap located at the end of this chapter. You will want to refer to this roadmap frequently for guidance and inspiration.

4. Congratulations! You have awakened your dreamer and created a powerful Vision Board. Now, select a special place in your home or office to display your Vision Board. In the coming weeks, refer to the activities you have completed in your vision notebook and review the questions you answered as your journey unfolds. Remember, it is good to live in the question.

Destined For Success
Achieving My Vision Goals
And What I Want In Life

My roadmap for my Vision Board created in association with
Chapter Ten, Awaken The Dreamer Within

Vision Board title:

Vision Board date:

Vision Description (state in present tense and describe what is represented on your Vision Board):

Who will benefit as a result my vision:

What achieving my vision will mean for my life:

What I am most excited about as I look at my vision for my future:

Date by which I want to achieve my vision:

Why my vision needs to happen:

How I will know that I have achieved my vision:

Let the Festivities Begin!

The four easiest steps in achieving my vision:

1. _____

2. _____

3. _____

4. _____

The very first step I will take toward my vision:

Where I need the greatest help or inspiration in achieving my vision:

Five things I can do in the next thirty days to move toward my vision:

1. _____

2. _____

3. _____

4. _____

5. _____

Five people who can help me in the next thirty days to move toward my vision:

1. _____

2. _____

3. _____

4. _____

5. _____

Five day to day things I can delegate to others within the next thirty days so that I can accelerate my journey toward my vision:

1. _____

2. _____

3. _____

4. _____

5. _____

Five time-barriers I can eliminate from my life in the next thirty days so that I have more time to devote to my goals:

1.

2.

3.

4.

5.

Three habits I can develop in the next sixty days to help me have greater positive energy to direct toward my vision:

1.

2.

3.

Three things I have never asked for that I am willing to request within the next sixty days in order to move toward my vision:

1.

2.

3.

Three ways to increase my prosperity and abundance in the next ninety days:

1. ....

2. ....

3. ....

One promise I will make to myself as I begin my journey toward my vision:

Chapter Eleven

Great Expectations

"I'm George"

Have you looked at a favorite photo of yourself lately? What is it about that photo that makes you smile? What memories does that photo conjure up for you?

For me, the photo above is my favorite childhood photo. I remember that hot summer day in 1966 as if it were yesterday. My playschool teachers loved that my friends and I went to "dress up day" as The Beatles. The band was all the rage, and my mother's keen costuming capabilities locked in the certainty that I would carry home a first place ribbon. What I love as much as the outfit with me in my skinny little Danskin leggings with a seam in front, is how my genuine happiness shows through in the photo. I was really living in a glorious moment in that photo, as George Harrison!

I feel fortunate that I am as authentically excited about possibilities in life today as I was when I was five. In my work, I connect with people and businesses to help them build their vision for a bigger and brighter future.

As you look at the life you are living today; family, career, relationship and location; is it your happiest time in your life, or do you need to increase your happiness?

Right now is when you begin to build a better, happier, more fulfilling and abundant life. Even if you are dissatisfied with your achievements, marriage, relationship status, health, or finances, there are probably many good things happening for you *right now* that you do not consider in your overall happiness score.

How excited are you about life's possibilities? It is possible that as you read this book, you are emerging from an experience of challenge or overcoming obstacles. Creating a habit of positive expectations takes practice and discipline. Practice the habit of positive expectations for just five minutes per day. It may not feel natural at first, but keep at it. Soon, it will feel comfortable and familiar and you will be on your way to *great* expectations.

Chapter Activity
Setting Positive Expectations

This activity is a practical, 45-minute energy shifting process designed for you to sit in a place of gratitude and neutrality. During this activity, you will set positive expectations for your future that will be reflected on your Vision Board. Keep in mind that our perspectives on life and possibility are constantly changing. You may wish to repeat this exercise each time you embark on a new Vision Board.

1. Gather the tools and materials you will need to create a Vision Board (See Chapter Seven). You will create the board at the conclusion of this activity. You will use the notes and scenarios you create in this activity to define the tone of your Vision Board and the pictures and phrases you place on it.

2. Set a timer for 30 minutes. During this time, you will focus on what is good or beneficial in your life today. Go to the internet and listen to inspiring/energetic music that puts you in a good mood, watch inspirational videos on YouTube, write in your journal, pull out old letters, birthday cards or notes wishing you good luck or congratulations on a new job, and surf the web for stories of inspiration of people who have overcome obstacles. Your goal in this exercise is to increase your feeling of hope and optimism.

3. After 30 minutes of focusing your energy, create a list, in the space below, of your talents, skills, and accomplishments. Compliment yourself. This list is for you. No one else will see it, so you do not need to worry about being humble. You know better than anyone, the ways in which you excel. You are likely better than anyone you know at some things. This is not the time for you to underestimate the value of your past in building the future of your dreams. This list is like a pep talk. You should make a copy of this list to keep in your purse or wallet as ongoing inspiration.

My Talents:

My Skills:

My Accomplishments:

Activities and Decision with which I would like assistance:

People who I can ask to assist me in achieving my goal:

4. Once you have completed your list, indulge your fantasy. Imagine people offering a helping hand on your road to success and a more fulfilling life. In the space below, list the things with which you would like assistance to speed you on your journey, naming the people from whom you would like help. You may not personally know all of the people on the list. That is okay. This is a fantasy. As I often say, thoughts are things. Think BIG. Be daring in your imagining.

5. Write a scenario, in the space below, in which the people who can influence your future in a positive way have assisted you with your request. There is magic in writing this scenario. Once you have imagined these people helping you, you have pictured the possibility and felt the positive results of their assistance. You also have a plan set in motion of the ways in which their agreement to assist you might play itself out. Write this scenario using the present tense, as if it is already happening. Be specific and include details.

My ideal scenario:

6. Now that you have shifted your energy, and you have a picture of what success and support look like for you, it is time to create your Vision Board! Find images that resemble people helping others in ways that relate to your vision of the future. Select, create, paste

together, and write phrases of encouragement. You will find dozens of phrases you can use in my Powerful Word Packs. They are located at www.buildingapowerfulvisionboard.com/forms Password: **possibilities**.

Layer your Vision Board with boldness. Be sure to include WOW! statements as you work. Phrases such as A Force To Be Reckoned With, Star Of The Show, and Stunningly Great are examples of WOW! statements. Your board, when completed, will emanate hope and positive expectation.

7. Attach the lists and scenarios you completed in this activity beside or on the back of your board.

8. Complete the *Destined for Success* Roadmap. The roadmap is located at the end of this chapter. You will want to refer to this roadmap frequently for guidance and inspiration.

9. Once each week, review the lists, scenarios, and *Destined For Success* roadmap. Reflect on the board and the roadmap. Engaging in this discipline will reignite your sense of possibility, and keep you moving in the direction of your dreams. It provides an opportunity to take note of the positive changes happening in your life.

Destined For Success
Achieving My Vision Goals
And What I Want In Life

My roadmap for my Vision Board created in association with
Chapter Eleven, Great Expectations

Vision Board title:

Vision Board date:

Vision Description (state in present tense and describe what is represented on your Vision Board):

Who will benefit as a result my vision:

What achieving my vision will mean for my life:

What I am most excited about as I look at my vision for my future:

Date by which I want to achieve my vision:

Why my vision needs to happen:

How I will know that I have achieved my vision:

Let the Festivities Begin!

The four easiest steps in achieving my vision:

1. _____

2. _____

3. _____

4. _____

The very first step I will take toward my vision:

Where I need the greatest help or inspiration in achieving my vision:

Five things I can do in the next thirty days to move toward my vision:

1.

2.

3.

4.

5.

Five people who can help me in the next thirty days to move toward my vision:

1.

2.

3.

4.

5.

Five day to day things I can delegate to others within the next thirty days so that I can accelerate my journey toward my vision:

1.

2.

3.

4.

5.

Five time-barriers I can eliminate from my life in the next thirty days so that I have more time to devote to my goals:

1. _____

2. _____

3. _____

4. _____

5. _____

Three habits I can develop in the next sixty days to help me have greater positive energy to direct toward my vision:

1. _____

2. _____

3. _____

Three things I have never asked for that I am willing to request within the next sixty days in order to move toward my vision:

1. _____

2. _____

3. _____

Three ways to increase my prosperity and abundance in the next ninety days:

1. ....

2. ....

3. ....

One promise I will make to myself as I begin my journey toward my vision:

Chapter Twelve

See The Outcome…Thoughts Are Things

Nearly ten years ago, I relocated to Indiana from Kentucky. A few months after purchasing our house in Indiana, I recalled a dream house wish list I had created two years earlier, but had since forgotten. One sunny day, I was driving along the Ohio River, admiring all of the lovely homes that overlooked the river. I started thinking about everything I wanted in a house. As I envisioned the details of my dream house, I imagined that it would be set back from the road, with trees all around it, and be on a body of water.

My dream house would include a large front window. Through that window, I would be able to see water in the background, perhaps a lake, or a river. I imagined spending lots of time on the water. The house would have plenty of room for entertaining, and there would be windows and sunlight along the back. My dream house would also have a fireplace that could be seen through the front window. There would be plenty of private spaces where family and friends who came to visit could work, read, chat, play, or be alone.

As I was doing some landscaping in front of our new house in Indiana, I suddenly noticed that as I looked through the front window, I could see the fireplace on the right hand side in the den. The sunroom had 21 windows through which sunlight streamed all day long. Through these windows, I could see the pool. As I gazed into my house from the outside, I had an Aha! moment. A rush of recognition came over me. *I was living in my dream house!* All of the elements of the vision I had created on that river road in Kentucky were present in our Indiana home: Eighteen trees, a body of water, set back from the road, with many private spaces and many windows. I was astonished.

My experience proves that even if you forget what you imagined and intended, time invested aligning desire and vision delivers powerful results. As you begin getting consistent results from your Vision Boards, your belief in what is possible will grow stronger.

It is often said, "You have to see it to believe it". There is much truth to this statement and it is an apt description of the process of creating a Vision Board. Imagination is what transforms our ideas into reality. When you get the idea to find a new job, new home, start a business, seek a new relationship, or have radiant health, your imagination comes alive. As we imagine, our minds wander in countless directions. Capture your positive thoughts and discard negative thoughts. Developing the habit of holding onto positive thoughts and feelings is paramount to setting positive expectations that lead to successful outcomes.

Chapter Activity
See Your *Future* As *Now*

You have probably been waiting longer than you expected to get what you want in life. See Your Future as Now is an activity designed to let you have the sensory experience of having achieved your desired result right now. It provides you with an immediate sample of how your future will feel. We will do this by acting "as if" your future is happening in this very moment. It will strengthen your connection to the outcomes you desire for your life.

1. Gather the tools and materials you will need to create a Vision Board (See Chapter Seven). You will create your board at the conclusion of this activity. You will use the colorful and detailed description of your future that you create in this activity to create a powerful board that includes you in the picture, surrounded by good things happening to you. To be sure that you are in your picture of the future, keep some photos of yourself nearby that you can paste on your board.

2. In the space below, describe your preferred future. Rather than writing future statements, write present tense statements, as if you are living your future NOW. Some call this acting "as if". You do not need to expend energy on every detail of how you got to your future. This same technique is used in improvisational comedy. The actors are directed to be in the moment, and not worry about what happened to their characters before the scene started or what lies in the future.

   Suspend your judgment. Go to your future NOW. Describe what it looks, feels and sounds like to have already achieved the celebrity, financial success, radiant health, travel and life goals that seemed far away and out of reach just a few minutes ago.

   As I look at the future I have created for myself, here is what my life is like:

3. Review what you have written about your future. Then, in the space below, rewrite your description of the future. Include yourself in the picture. Move from a place of observation to a place of participation. Become part of the landscape and the experience.

59

Build on the description statements in the list above. Begin your descriptive statement with "I am". Your statements will be bolder and more grounded. There is an increase in confidence that results from strength statements. "I am" statements are much stronger and more resilient than "I wish" statements.

As I now live the future I created for myself, I am:

Destined For Success
Achieving My Vision Goals
And What I Want In Life

My roadmap for my Vision Board created in association with
Chapter Twelve, See The Outcome....Thoughts Are Things

Vision Board title:

Vision Board date:

Vision Description (state in present tense and describe what is represented on your Vision Board):

Who will benefit as a result my vision:

What achieving my vision will mean for my life:

What I am most excited about as I look at my vision for my future:

Date by which I want to achieve my vision:

Why my vision needs to happen:

How I will know that I have achieved my vision:

61

Let the Festivities Begin!

The four easiest steps in achieving my vision:

1. _____

2. _____

3. _____

4. _____

The very first step I will take toward my vision:

Where I need the greatest help or inspiration in achieving my vision:

Five things I can do in the next thirty days to move toward my vision:

1. _____

2. _____

3. _____

4. _____

5. _____

Five people who can help me in the next thirty days to move toward my vision:

1. _____

2. _____

3. _____

4. _____

5. _____

Five day to day things I can delegate to others within the next thirty days so that I can accelerate my journey toward my vision:

1. _____

2. _____

3. _____

4. _____

5. _____

Five time-barriers I can eliminate from my life in the next thirty days so that I have more time to devote to my goals:

1. _____

2. _____

3. _____

4. _____

5. _____

Three habits I can develop in the next sixty days to help me have greater positive energy to direct toward my vision:

1. _____

2. _____

3. _____

Three things I have never asked for that I am willing to request within the next sixty days in order to move toward my vision:

1. _____

2. _____

3. _____

Three ways to increase my prosperity and abundance in the next ninety days:

1. _____

2. _____

3. _____

One promise I will make to myself as I begin my journey toward my vision:

Chapter Thirteen

Nice And Easy Does It, Every Time

I approach projects with zeal. One summer, I decided that we should grow our own produce. My husband helped me set up a garden box near our tool shed. I was determined to experience grand success as an agricultural novice. In my 8 x 8 foot patch, I planted lettuce, strawberries, carrots, eggplant, pumpkins, tomato plants, and a grapevine. I decided that perhaps I could start a vineyard on the chicken wire surrounding the patch and really optimize the space and make wine in the future.

A friend who is a veteran gardener was quite amused when she came over to our house for a party and I proudly showed her my farm in the yard. I am sure that my pack-it-all-in approach to gardening offered her some insight into my approach to life and work. I want it all, and I want it now! She recommended that I thin out my garden, because I was going to choke the growth of any single crop by trying to fit so much into one small space.

My early gardening experience taught me a lesson: You do not have to pack your request for everything you want in your entire life all at once. Sometimes, focusing on one, two, or three items or outcomes at a time yields a better harvest.

You may think that if you pack all of your ideas for success into one single Vision Board, more things will happen quickly for you. While a full and varied board is filled with energy, delight, and a zest for life, you may want to create a series of Vision Boards. You do not have to limit yourself to one Vision Board. You can choose just one area of life or one situation on which you would like to concentrate. By taking this approach, you can add detail that you might not be able to include in a general board. Artists will often spend a number of months or years on one particular theme. Sometimes, less is more. Make it easy on yourself and on the Universe to deliver your results!

Chapter Activity
Single Point of Concentration (SPOC)

The purpose of this activity is to de-clutter your mind, to sort and to separate aspects of your vision for your life by taking the approach of "divide and conquer". You will select one area on which to focus your attention. You will enrich the detail of your vision for a single goal or achievement you seek.

1. Gather the tools and materials you will need to create a Vision Board (See Chapter Seven). You will create a Vision Board focused on one goal or key area of your life at the conclusion of this activity. If you plan to do a series of single-focus Vision Boards, you may want to decide in advance if you would like the dimensions of your various boards to be the same or make each topical board unique.

2. Give yourself the luxury of indulging in some solitary thinking for a few minutes. There are probably dozens of things that you would like to improve, change, or achieve, and each is competing for your attention. Simplify your thinking. In the space below, list the five things you most want to receive or change in your life in the next year. Then, prioritize the five things you most want.

1. _____
2. _____
3. _____
4. _____
5. _____

3. Write a statement in the space below that describes how you would like your number one priority to be present in your work or life 180 days from now.

How I'd like my life to look 6 months from today:

4. Set a timer for 30 minutes and browse the Internet for information, insight, pictures and quotes related to your top priority. Print as you go. Do not spend more than a few minutes on any one site, unless it is a gold mine. Even if it is, move on after five minutes.

5. At the conclusion of your 30-minute session, review what you have compiled and printed. You will feel educated, refreshed, informed, and very connected to your goal.

6. Add to the pictures and phrases you have selected on the Internet by browsing through magazines and selecting phrases from my Powerful Word Packs. You can download the Powerful Word Packs at www.buildingapowerfulvisionboard.com/forms
    Password: **possibilities**.

7. Assemble your materials on your Vision Board. As you create your Vision Board, make a mental note of how good it feels to have indulged in focusing on just one desire, one goal. It provides the opportunity to think of more ways to fulfill that goal. It also gives you time and space to imagine what life will be like when you achieve your priority goal. The luxury of thinking about one thing only is like a mini-retreat for your soul.

8. Reflect on what you have created in this activity, and make some reflection notes on the back of this activity sheet. Notice your degree of clarity, your confidence level, and your belief in the possibility of achieving the goal on which you have focused.

9. Complete the Destined for Success Roadmap. The roadmap is located at the end of this chapter. You will want to refer to this roadmap frequently for guidance and inspiration.

10. Write the date on your project and find a special place to display your Vision Board. Visit your "S.P.O.C." (Single Point of Concentration) project every day.

Repeat this Vision Board exercise once a week with your four remaining top priorities. When you have completed all five Vision Boards, you will have a gallery of possibility surrounding you, to guide you on your journey to the life of your dreams!

Destined For Success
Achieving My Vision Goals
And What I Want In Life

My roadmap for my Vision Board created in association with
Chapter Thirteen, Nice And Easy Does It, Every Time

Vision Board title:

Vision Board date:

Vision Description (state in present tense and describe what is represented on your Vision Board):

Who will benefit as a result my vision:

What achieving my vision will mean for my life:

What I am most excited about as I look at my vision for my future:

Date by which I want to achieve my vision:

Why my vision needs to happen:

How I will know that I have achieved my vision:

Let the Festivities Begin!

The four easiest steps in achieving my vision:

1. ....

2. ....

3. ....

4. ....

The very first step I will take toward my vision:

Where I need the greatest help or inspiration in achieving my vision:

Five things I can do in the next thirty days to move toward my vision:

1. ....

2. ....

3. ....

4. ....

5. ....

Five people who can help me in the next thirty days to move toward my vision:

1. ....

2. ....

3. ....

4. ....

5. ....

Five day to day things I can delegate to others within the next thirty days so that I can accelerate my journey toward my vision:

1. ....

2. ....

3. ....

4. ....

5. ....

Five time-barriers I can eliminate from my life in the next thirty days so that I have more time to devote to my goals:

1.

2.

3.

4.

5.

Three habits I can develop in the next sixty days to help me have greater positive energy to direct toward my vision:

1.

2.

3.

Three things I have never asked for that I am willing to request within the next sixty days in order to move toward my vision:

1.

2.

3.

Three ways to increase my prosperity and abundance in the next ninety days:

1.

2.

3.

One promise I will make to myself as I begin my journey toward my vision:

Chapter Fourteen

Secret Agent Plan!

What is it about spy films that keep us headed to the theater for buckets of popcorn, gallons of soda and mounds of chocolate? Is it the thrill of the chase and the plots filled with invincible heroes? When we watch spy movies, we imagine that we are crafty and daring enough to live a life of intrigue and suspense. I would love to be a secret agent. The secret agent lifestyle includes mystery, intrigue, and excitement.

Here is your opportunity to live a daring life: While you are busy being all things to all people, you can create a vision for your future that can sit innocently on your desk or be posted on your wall that will work as your secret agent in the background. Who would know that only you can decipher your collage of pictures, and that it is your powerful weapon for success?

Similar to a monthly calendar, you can have an active Vision Board in front of you for the 40, 50 or 70 hours a week that you are working. If you are a road warrior, keep your agent in your planner or portfolio. Investing a few hours each month in creating a visual plan for where you see yourself in the future will amaze you.

Your mission, should you choose to accept it, is to follow the instructions on the following page exactly. You can wear a trench coat while you complete the mission, but that is purely optional. People might get suspicious if you sit in a room with scissors, a glue stick and poster board while wearing a trench coat. They will think you are writing a ransom note. You had better forget the coat. Just do the exercise.

Chapter Activity
The Details of the Plan

The purpose of this activity is to provide an illustration of the goals you wish to achieve in the next year, categorized by number of days to achievement.

1. Gather the tools and materials you will need to create a Vision Board (See Chapter Seven).

2. In the space below, make a list of what you would like to achieve in the next year.

    In the area of career, one year from now, I want to have...

    In the area of relationship, one year from now, I want to be...

    In the area of finance, one year from now, I want to have accomplished...

    In the area of contribution to the world, I want to be...

3. Browse magazines. Head to the Internet to find photos, quotes, and phrases that vividly illustrate what you want in your life.

4. Put a timeframe on each of the goals you would like to achieve. Use timeframes of 90, 180 and 365 days.

5. Group the pictures, quotes and phrases you have gathered according to these timeframes.

6. It is now time to create your strategic Vision Board. Write the numbers 90, 180 and 365 on your board. Paste your pictures, quotes and phrases around their corresponding number.

7. Take photos of your board. Strategically place these photos in three places:

   a. In an 8.5 X 11 frame for your desk

   b. As a screen saver or background for your computer

   c. As the background on your cell phone

8. Set a monthly appointment in your calendar to review your board and track your progress. You will be amazed by how much progress you can make in just a few months. Keep a notebook and make some notes about your progress. It will provide a great record of what you were thinking month by month when you look back on it.

9. Complete the *Destined for Success* Roadmap. The roadmap is located at the end of this chapter. You will want to refer to this roadmap frequently for guidance and inspiration.

Here is the best part... You are your own secret agent of change!

Destined For Success
Achieving My Vision Goals
And What I Want In Life

My roadmap for my Vision Board created in association with
Chapter Fourteen, Secret Agent Plan!

Vision Board title:

Vision Board date:

Vision Description (state in present tense and describe what is represented on your Vision Board):

Who will benefit as a result my vision:

What achieving my vision will mean for my life:

What I am most excited about as I look at my vision for my future:

Date by which I want to achieve my vision:

Why my vision needs to happen:

How I will know that I have achieved my vision:

Let the Festivities Begin!

The four easiest steps in achieving my vision:

1. _____

2. _____

3. _____

4. _____

The very first step I will take toward my vision:

Where I need the greatest help or inspiration in achieving my vision:

Five things I can do in the next thirty days to move toward my vision:

1. ....

2. ....

3. ....

4. ....

5. ....

Five people who can help me in the next thirty days to move toward my vision:

1. ....

2. ....

3. ....

4. ....

5. ....

Five day to day things I can delegate to others within the next thirty days so that I can accelerate my journey toward my vision:

1. ....

2. ....

3. ....

4. ....

5. ....

Five time-barriers I can eliminate from my life in the next thirty days so that I have more time to devote to my goals:

1.
2.
3.
4.
5.

Three habits I can develop in the next sixty days to help me have greater positive energy to direct toward my vision:

1.
2.
3.

Three things I have never asked for that I am willing to request within the next sixty days in order to move toward my vision:

1.
2.
3.

Three ways to increase my prosperity and abundance in the next ninety days:

1.
2.
3.

One promise I will make to myself as I begin my journey toward my vision:

Chapter Fifteen

Abundant Thinking

I was raised to be polite, share, to only take my portion and leave some for others. Somewhere along the line, I also picked up the message, "Don't Get Your Hopes Up". When we approach life from the perspective that in order for one person to gain, another person must lose, we are cutting off possibility and the flow of abundance from ourselves and from others. Your Vision Board can help you change your mindset about abundance.

I figured out a few years ago that building a Vision Board is like going to an *All You Can Eat* restaurant. You can have as many servings of possibility with your Vision Board as you can helpings of mashed potatoes or dessert at a buffet. You do not have to be reasonable as you write out and put into picture what you want in your life. Think abundantly!

When I created what I call my Universe Catalog a few years ago, I gave myself permission to ask for anything I wanted. I suspended thoughts about how my busy career would limit the amount of time and resources I had to pursue an entrepreneurial venture. In that moment, I decided to act as the CEO of my life, telling my team about new product development, marketing ideas and financial results I expected for my new venture. It was simply exhilarating. By being adventurous and thinking abundantly, I made the transition from employee to company owner in less than two years! I have products, workshops, and a publishing venture.

Now is your time to think abundantly and give yourself permission to ask for anything you want. Think about what you are looking to achieve relative to your career, travel, or contribution to your community. Are you feasting on possibility, constantly adding to your picture and description of what you would like in life or are you daintily selecting just a few morsels? There is no harm in being bold. Remember that when you are building your vision, abundance is the order of the day.

Chapter Activity
Taking Abundant Thinking to a Conscious Level

The purpose of this activity is to activate abundant thinking. This is an ideal activity for people who have difficulty believing that they deserve abundance or have difficulty asking for what they want in life. For readers accustomed to "just getting by", this may feel like a stretch. Stay with it!

1. Gather the tools and materials you will need to create your Vision Board (See Chapter Seven).

2. In the space below, write a statement describing what you want to own, to do and have. Include the topics of family, career, home, vacation, volunteerism and health.

    My radiant life is a vision to behold! Here is what it includes:

3. Rewrite your statement, making it bigger and bolder, and asking for more. If limiting self-talk bubbles up, immediately release it. For example, if you wrote a statement about having $1 million dollars during Step 2, stretch your imagination during this rewrite. Envision being a multimillionaire. Once you have completed your rewrite, compare the two statements. It is likely that your second statement is grander than the first.

My radiant life is a vision to behold! It is rich with all of the following:

4. Make notes in the margins of this activity sheet about how having your grander statement materialize can take your life and personal effectiveness to a higher level. Spend a few minutes reflecting on your notes. If you find yourself thinking that you are asking for too much, suspend self-judgment.

5. Now, it is time to create a Vision Board that declares the abundance you want in your life. Your Vision Board is a "no apologies" zone. It is a safe place to ask for what you want. Using the statement you created in Step 3 as a guide, select pictures and phrases that vividly describe and illustrate your vision. This project is an ideal opportunity to use the Powerful Word Packs.
You can download the Word Packs at:
www.buildingapowerfulvisionboard.com/forms
Password: **possibilities**. Be bold in your choices!

6. Once you have completed your Vision Board, consider framing it and placing it in a negativity-free zone in your home. If you are at all shy about displaying this board, take photos of the board and use them as the desktop background on your computer or as the background on your cell phone.

7. If sustaining your belief in the fact that you deserve abundance is a challenge for you, visit your Vision Board often. It will help you stay connected to what you are seeking to attract into your life, and will speed the process of what you want coming into your life.

8. Complete the *Destined for Success Roadmap* for this chapter. It is located at the end of this chapter. You will want to refer to this roadmap frequently for guidance and inspiration.

Destined For Success
Achieving My Vision Goals
And What I Want In Life

My roadmap for my Vision Board created in association with
Chapter Fifteen, Abundant Thinking

Vision Board title:

Vision Board date:

Vision Description (state in present tense and describe what is represented on your Vision Board):

Who will benefit as a result my vision:

What achieving my vision will mean for my life:

What I am most excited about as I look at my vision for my future:

Date by which I want to achieve my vision:

Why my vision needs to happen:

How I will know that I have achieved my vision:

Let the Festivities Begin!

The four easiest steps in achieving my vision:

1. _____

2. _____

3. _____

4. _____

The very first step I will take toward my vision:

Where I need the greatest help or inspiration in achieving my vision:

Five things I can do in the next thirty days to move toward my vision:

1. _____

2. _____

3. _____

4. _____

5. _____

Five people who can help me in the next thirty days to move toward my vision:

1. _____

2. _____

3. _____

4. _____

5. _____

Five day to day things I can delegate to others within the next thirty days so that I can accelerate my journey toward my vision:

1. _____

2. _____

3. _____

4. _____

5. _____

Five time-barriers I can eliminate from my life in the next thirty days so that I have more time to devote to my goals:

1. ....

2. ....

3. ....

4. ....

5. ....

Three habits I can develop in the next sixty days to help me have greater positive energy to direct toward my vision:

1. ....

2. ....

3. ....

Three things I have never asked for that I am willing to request within the next sixty days in order to move toward my vision:

1. ....

2. ....

3. ....

Three ways to increase my prosperity and abundance in the next ninety days:

1. ....

2. ....

3. ....

One promise I will make to myself as I begin my journey toward my vision:

Chapter Sixteen

Stake Your Claim

When I read the words "Stake Your Claim", I envision a skinny little man with an overloaded pack mule putting a sign in the ground to show the world that a plot of land in the Wild West belongs to him. I see him, hat in hand, dancing and laughing like a wild man. That sort of excitement is over the top and that little caricature of a man leaves me with a feeling of excitement and possibility. I can hear him now, telling everyone who tries to squelch his dreams that, "There's gold in them thar hills!"

Your Vision Board can be as brave and mouthy as the little man who is panning for gold. Your Vision Board is your chance to stake your claim and create a shift in your thinking.

Strength statements on your Vision Board are most powerful when they are stated in present tense and action based terms. Examples of these terms include; "Best in Class", "In a League of Her Own", "Master of his Craft", "A Force To Be Reckoned With", "Brilliant", and "Unparalleled". What you will not find on a powerful Vision Board are the following phrases: "I really hope that....", "What I really want to have is...." or "I'm sort of afraid to say it out loud, but..."

When you write a career objective as a header on your resume, you give it confidence and clarity. You use terms such as excellent, outstanding, and best in class. You would not write a career objective that reads, "To pursue a career with a reasonably functional company, where I can occasionally contribute to the overall productivity and growth of the organization". You would not sabotage yourself by placing limiting statements on your resume. A career objective proclaims your talents, skills, and accomplishments. So does a Vision Board. It is a picture of the life you will create. That life will result from your unique talents, your combination of skills and accomplishments from your life.

It is your time and your turn to Stake Your Claim! In preparation for building a powerful Vision Board, this next activity will help you recall and herald the gifts and experiences that will contribute to your bright future. At the conclusion of the activity, you will create a strength-centered Vision Board that can help you confidently claim your future.

Chapter Activity
Claim your Strengths and Talents

The purpose of this activity is to build belief in your strengths and talents, and to provide you with evidence that you can truly claim your right to live a life you love. This activity is a confidence builder that will help you become your own biggest fan.

This is a two-phased activity. You will complete the first four steps today, and then return to create your Vision Board one week later.

1. Gather the tools and materials you will need to create your Vision Board (See Chapter Seven). You will be using index cards to create your claim checks.

2. Grab a stack of 10 note cards. These will be your claim checks. On the front of each claim check, write a simple statement about one talent, capability, or strength. Leave room for a picture. Even if you hesitate to write out some of your strengths and talents because you might doubt yourself a bit, write the statement anyway. Many strengths and talents are a work in progress.

3. Find a picture or quote that illustrates or connects you to each of your ten claim checks. Paste the pictures and quotes on the corresponding claim checks.

4. On the back of each claim check, make a numbered list, 1 through 7.

5. Lay your 10 claim checks in front of you so that you can review your talents as a set. If there are claim checks that you are tempted to hide at the bottom of the stack, make a mark in their upper right hand corner. This will serve as your reminder about the strength statements to which you will want to give some special attention so that they become stronger.

6. Put a rubber band around your claim checks or put them in a small case. Place your claim checks in your briefcase or purse. Carry your claim checks with you for the next week. At some point each day, give yourself a five-minute head start on your way to a meeting, lunch, or picking up the kids. With those five minutes, review your claim checks, noting one way in which that stated strength is being used in your day-to-day activities. This will validate your conviction about your abilities. In just one week, you will have compiled 70 concrete examples of your talents, strengths and capabilities.

One week later:

It is now time to build your Vision Board. Take ten minutes to review your 10 claim checks, noting the ways in which your strengths and talents are at work in your life. After you have reviewed your claim checks, create a Vision Board that declares your strengths and talents. Include each of your strength statements on the board. Surround the strength statements on your board with pictures that illustrate what those strengths will help you attract into your life.

Note: If you liked the deck of cards concept from last week's activity, you might prefer to make a deck of vision cards rather than a Vision Board for this project. Include strength comments and pictures of the dynamic life that these strength comments will help you achieve. You can review them one at a time, or lay them out to make a collective picture that can be sorted, shuffled or grouped into a variety of patterns and themes.

1. Complete the *Destined for Success* Roadmap for this exercise. It is located at the end of this chapter. You will want to refer to this roadmap frequently for guidance and inspiration.

2. Display your Vision Board in the room where you do most of your reflective thinking. Seeing your Vision Board each day will serve as a reminder that you are a successful and capable attractor of what you want in life.

Destined For Success
Achieving My Vision Goals
And What I Want In Life

My roadmap for my Vision Board created in association with
Chapter Sixteen, Stake Your Claim

Vision Board title:

Vision Board date:

Vision Description (state in present tense and describe what is represented on your Vision Board):

Who will benefit as a result my vision:

What achieving my vision will mean for my life:

What I am most excited about as I look at my vision for my future:

Date by which I want to achieve my vision:

Why my vision needs to happen:

How I will know that I have achieved my vision:

Let the Festivities Begin!

The four easiest steps in achieving my vision:

1. _____

2. _____

3. _____

4. _____

The very first step I will take toward my vision:

Where I need the greatest help or inspiration in achieving my vision:

Five things I can do in the next thirty days to move toward my vision:

1. ....

2. ....

3. ....

4. ....

5. ....

Five people who can help me in the next thirty days to move toward my vision:

1. ....

2. ....

3. ....

4. ....

5. ....

Five day to day things I can delegate to others within the next thirty days so that I can accelerate my journey toward my vision:

1. ....

2. ....

3. ....

4. ....

5. ....

Five time-barriers I can eliminate from my life in the next thirty days so that I have more time to devote to my goals:

1.
2.
3.
4.
5.

Three habits I can develop in the next sixty days to help me have greater positive energy to direct toward my vision:

1.
2.
3.

Three things I have never asked for that I am willing to request within the next sixty days in order to move toward my vision:

1.
2.
3.

Three ways to increase my prosperity and abundance in the next ninety days:

1. ....

2. ....

3. ....

One promise I will make to myself as I begin my journey toward my vision:

Chapter Seventeen

You Are The Chairman of The Board for Your Future

A move from Chicago to Kansas City in 1992 changed the course of my life. I trusted my intuition and took a leap of faith that stepping out of my comfort zone to review and renew my direction would bring new opportunities and adventures. I was at a crossroads in my life. I had been toggling between work in higher education and the pursuit of a theater career since graduating from college. The decision to strike out on my own made all the difference in my journey.

I left family, friends, and certainty. I loaded all of my belongings into a 10-foot rental truck, drove to Kansas City with a friend, and started a new chapter in my life. I had no job and my closest acquaintance lived 75 miles away. The move was the start of a nine-year adventure in risk, discovery, growth, and clarity.

My great adventure was not without trials and tribulations. There were many times during my first two years that I lived in Kansas City when I needed advice, encouragement, and wisdom. In the absence of any nearby advisors, my thoughts turned to the advice that the people who had inspired me or influenced my life and my development would offer in challenging times. I called this imaginary group my *Board of Advisors*.

Seated at my boardroom table were my childhood idol Carol Burnett, diplomat and inventor Ben Franklin, financial genius Warren Buffet, savvy single girl icon of the silver screen Katherine Hepburn, writer and champion of triumph of the spirit Nora Ephron, and my Campfire leader Martha Albee. They have each left a mark on my life in some way.

I selected these people to represent wise parts of my own experience and perspective: diligence, brilliance, creativity, and tenacity. Whether or not I knew each one personally, each possessed qualities I admired. Some were challenging, some were supportive, some offered common sense, and all were smart!

Creating a council of ever-present advisors provides an emotional boost and reassurance as you build your business or personal future and advance toward your goals. Who challenged you to be bolder, kinder, more studious, or more tenacious? Whose biography have you read time and again? What historical figures do you most admire? Who is your favorite movie character? Who is your business idol? These lifetime influencing favorites can be with you, front and center. It is as simple as creating a collage that you keep at your desk or on your wall to remind you that you are a composite of your experiences and what you have learned.

Chapter Activity
Create Your Board of Advisors

Today, you will assign your Board of Advisors. You will consciously tap into sources of inspiration from your life, as well as access the perspectives of great thinkers past and present. This activity will help you develop a discipline of looking at a problem from many points of view. The perspective of your Board of Advisors, coupled with your own experience, will make you a better problem solver.

1. Gather the tools and materials you will need to create your Vision Board (See Chapter Seven).

2. In the space below, make a list of the people who have had a significant positive impact on your life. Next to each person's name, describe a key life lesson or perspective you received from him or her.

   Name   Key Life Lesson

3. Make a list of favorite books and movies, noting key characters or messages from the works that have influenced your life.

   Title   Key Character or Message

4. Make a list of religious or spiritual leaders who inspire you. For each leader you list, how has their key message made a difference in your life?

    Name   How Message Made A Difference

5. Make a list of the business and industry leaders you most admire. Why do you admire them?

    Name   Reason for Admiration

6. From the lists you have created, mark the names of those who would serve you well as an Advisor. Consider those who would prompt you to challenge the status quo, reach for new heights, reassure you in times of doubt and offer you good advice as you progress to your future. List the names of the people you chose in the space below, along with a statement of why you have selected each. You can take this exercise a step further by naming an Executive Committee. Who should be President, who should be Treasurer, etc?

    Advisor Name   Why Selected

7. Write one or two paragraphs describing the advice that your newly assigned *Board of Advisors* would offer you about how to achieve your goals, grow your business, or make a key decision in moving toward a happier life.

   Advice from my Board of Advisors:

8. Now that you have selected your *Board of Advisors*, you are ready to create two Vision Boards: one large, one small. On the larger board, combine the advice from Step 7 with pictures, photos, symbols or mementos that remind you of your selected advisors.

9. On the smaller board, create a group picture or mini-vision board that you can keep at your desk or in a place where you often seek inspiration.

10. Spend some quiet time with your completed picture. Consider the positive effect that the comprehensive wisdom of your *Board of Advisors* will have on your confidence and decision making skills.

11. Complete the *Destined for Success* Roadmap for this exercise. It is located at the end of this chapter. You will want to refer to this roadmap frequently for guidance and inspiration.

12. Proudly display your group picture. Frame it, and keep it in front of you. As you go through your day, pause and contemplate what this group would advise you to do.

<u>Destined For Success</u>
<u>Achieving My Vision Goals</u>
<u>And What I Want In Life</u>

My roadmap for my Vision Board created in association with
Chapter Seventeen, You Are The Chairman Of The Board For
Your Future

Vision Board title:

Vision Board date:

How I will benefit from accessing my *Board of Advisors*:

What I appreciate most about having my *Board of Advisors'* perspectives to turn to in times of challenge:

How tuning into the wisdom of my *Board of Advisors* will enable me to build a powerful future:

104

Let the Festivities Begin!

The first four pieces of advice I will ask of my *Board of Advisors*:

1. _____

2. _____

3. _____

4. _____

Where I need the greatest help or inspiration in creating a powerful future:

Three habits I can develop in the next sixty days to help me have greater positive energy to direct toward my future:

1. _____

2. _____

3. _____

Three people involved in my life from whom I will seek advice in the next sixty days:

1. _____

2. _____

3. _____

Three ways to increase my prosperity and abundance in the next ninety days:

1. _____

2. _____

3. _____

Five time-barriers I can eliminate from my life in the next thirty days so that I have more time to devote to my goals:

1. _____

2. _____

3. _____

4. _____

5. _____

Three habits I can develop in the next sixty days to help me have greater positive energy to direct toward my vision:

1. _____

2. _____

3. _____

Three things I have never asked for that I am willing to request within the next sixty days in order to move toward my vision:

1. _____

2. _____

3. _____

Three ways to increase my prosperity and abundance in the next ninety days:

1. ....

2. ....

3. ....

One promise I will make to myself as I begin my journey toward my vision:

Chapter Eighteen

Once Upon A Time...

I love the words, "Once upon a time". Growing up, I had the pleasure of being read to at night by my parents or by my older brothers and sisters. To this day, I love to read aloud and engage in storytelling.

Stories transport you to a place far, far away, or make you laugh or open your mind to new possibilities and horizons. As a child, I spent countless hours in the children's section of the library, reading dozens of books that expanded my sense of wonder. My early reading years provided a foundation for the sense of wonder, adventure, curiosity, and possibility that drive my life today.

Up to this point, the focus of our work book has been on the Vision Board – the outward facing, display board that you keep in front of you as you begin your quest toward your vision. Now that you are acquainted with the philosophy and methods of creating Vision Boards, you may wish to expand your toolset. Writing a future focused tale, your "Once Upon A Future" tale, is something you might enjoy and find effective. Writing a "Once Upon A Future" tale can provide a private and detailed alternative to creating a Vision Board.

Whether you shout your plans, hopes, and aspirations from a mountaintop or you keep them contained in a notebook is a personal preference. We each have a preferred manner of sharing or storing our dreams. The following exercise will help you get started with your "Once Upon A Future" Tale.

Chapter Activity
Getting Started With Your "Once upon a Future" Tale

What to do:

1. Go to a local bookstore or a public library. Spend an hour in the children's book section. Reacquaint yourself with "Once Upon A Time". This will help you connect with your imagination remind you of how fairy tales unfold.

2. Purchase a spiral notebook in which you will keep your *Once Upon A Future* journal. Select a notebook that you can fit into your briefcase or purse.

3. Immediately take 10 minutes in your car, at the subway station or at a coffee shop to initiate your journal. Give your journal a working title. I might name mine *Tess' Financial Freedom Journal* or *How Tess Created $280,000 Annual Income* or *Tess' Emancipation Documentation.* Once you have given your journal a title, write one or two paragraphs describing what *"Happily Ever After"* looks like to you.

4. Pick a date on which you will continue to write your *Once Upon A Future* tale. Name the topic on which you will write. By doing this, you are establishing a sense of importance and you are making an appointment for time devoted to your future. You are also giving yourself something to daydream about between today and the date of your next journaling session.

5. Place your journal into your briefcase or purse. Keeping your *Once Upon A Future* tale with you will serve as a reminder that your story is unfolding. I often pre-name chapters for the book I am writing, so that I do not experience writer's block. If I give myself the direction of a topic on which to write, I am able to be more productive during my work sessions. My edits may be many, but putting the pen to paper is easy when I have pre-planned entries.

6. Reread your journal entries from time to time. You will enjoy reading about your hopes, aspirations, and plans as much as you enjoy reading about the hopes and plans of characters from treasured childhood books.

Part Three
Recommendations, Resources and Additional Activities
Chapter Nineteen

Themed Vision Boards on Solo Topics

A Symphony or a Solo?
Per dictionary.com

sym·pho·ny: an elaborate instrumental composition in three or more movements, similar in form to a sonata but written for an orchestra and usually of far grander proportions and more varied elements.

so·lo: a musical composition or a passage or section in a musical composition written for performance by one singer or instrumentalist, with or without accompaniment: She sang a solo.

A Vision Board is typically a montage of ideas – filled with both words and pictures. Together, they create a symphony of ideas about how your future will unfold. Your Vision Board can be multi-themed to include your vision for career, love, business, and finance on one board.

However, there are times when only a solo will do and you want to build a Vision Board with just one theme. At a recent *Building A Powerful Vision Board* workshop, a participant shared with me that something was holding her back from completing her Vision Board. During our discussion, she discovered that each of her Vision Board themes was like an individual instrument that needed to be given a solo performance.

Once the participant determined that she wanted to create individually themed Vision Boards, she sorted the pictures and phrases she had selected and held onto months earlier by theme. Over the course of the next few hours, she created three separate Vision Boards. Once she completed her individually themed Vision Boards, her vision took on powerful clarity. Set side by side, her boards worked together like individual movements in a symphony. She was very happy with the outcome. She refers to these boards every day by using photos of each as her iPhone backgrounds.

In order to determine your preferred Vision Board style, and what sort of work setting invokes your greatest clarity and creativity, complete the following statement:

"I prefer…"

Working on projects in groups

Working alone

Communicating with words

Communicating with Pictures

Working with words and pictures blended together

Quiet while I work

Music and video while I work

Defining your work preferences and style will determine what sort of Vision Boards will be most effective in helping you advance toward your goals and achieve your ideal life!

Chapter Twenty

The Space Between Ask and Receive

I spent many years working in the restaurant industry while pursuing degrees and dreams. Long before owning a restaurant, I was a server and a short order cook. Between the ages of 15 and 35, I worked every job in a restaurant except dishwasher. Along the way, I learned that there is wisdom in restaurant work that can be applied to building a powerful Vision Board.

If you think about it, restaurants are magical. As the customer, you tell your server what you would like to have for dinner, and it is delivered to you, just as you asked.

A restaurant order is a simple and straightforward example of manifestation. Your server asks you what you would like to eat. You provide the details of your order so that it comes out in a manner that will make you happy. Your server writes the order on his pad and then takes it into the kitchen, where your meal is created. A short time later, your meal is delivered to you, fresh from the kitchen. If you have provided clear detail about your order, there is no confusion for the cook and you will be satisfied with what you are given.

Just as it is important for you to be clear and specific when you place an order at a restaurant, it is important to be specific when working with Vision Boards. Create a clear vision for your future. Choose images and phrases that illustrate specifically what you want. Then, let your Vision Board go to work preparing life's banquet for you.

Here is a guide to placing your order: Some restaurants offer an all-inclusive meal that includes an appetizer, a main course, a side items and a drink. Think of your Vision Board in the same way. Determine what will be the key focus of your Vision Board, as well as a few other categories of manifestation that you would like to include on your board. Create your Vision Board and then allow the Universe to deliver the order you have placed.

Enjoy the experience of your future unfolding. In keeping with the restaurant theme, compare it to dining out. Who enjoys being with someone who only asks, "When is my food going to get here? What's taking so long?" Dining out is not just about the order you placed. It is about the entire dining experience: Your surroundings, the music, the joy of being served, and discovering new flavors and dishes.

Give Back. Just as you leave a gratuity for your server, identify something that you can give back to the Universe in exchange for the bounty you receive!

Chapter Twenty-One

Ready, Set, Go!

"Don't wait until everything is just right. It will never be perfect. There will always be challenges, obstacles and less than perfect conditions. So what. Get started now. With each step you take, you will grow stronger and stronger, more and more skilled, more and more self-confident and more and more successful."

- Mark Victor Hansen

Each day contains the gift of 1440 minutes. Regardless of how busy your life is, save some precious time for yourself. The opening paragraph of *Building A Powerful Vision Board* states, "The life we believe we deserve is often the life we create." In working through the activities in the book and creating one or more Vision Boards, I hope that you have developed a strong conviction that you deserve an abundant and colorful life. My wish for you is that you create a life you love. Once you have imagined a bigger world, bolder relationships, and greater success, the results will begin.

Although you will close this book, keep your eyes open to possibility. You have awakened the dreamer within. As you continue on your journey, I encourage you to:

Broaden your horizons – try something new every day.
Take a new route to work.
Read.
Watch.
Listen.
Converse.
Contemplate.
Stay alert.
Build your sense of optimism.
Enhance negativity-free thinking.
Begin.
Begin again.
Surround yourself with positive people.
Commit.
Notice.
Ignore.
Forgive.
Do your homework.
Celebrate Small Wins.
Celebrate Big Wins.
Count to ten.
Appreciate what you already have.
Ask for more.
Live a life you love.
Whistle.
Choose happiness.
Be kinder than is necessary.
Assume that people act with good intentions.
Overpay at lemonade stands. A lemonade stand is usually a child's first exercise in attracting abundance.

It has been a pleasure creating *Building A Powerful Vision Board.* I hope that you live a life that is true to your purpose and that you achieve your goals and what you want in life!

Resource Guide
Tools To Support Your Journey to Your Future

Tess Denton's Tools for Creating and Sharing Your Vision Boards:

http://www.buildingapowerfulvisionboard.com
http://www.buildingapowerfulvisionboard.com/forms
Password: **possibilities**
http://www.buildingapowerfulvisionboard.wordpress.com

Books That Can Enrich Your Life:

Ask and it is Given by Jerry and Esther Hicks

Creative Visualization by Shakti Gawain

Chapters: Create a Life of Exhilaration and Accomplishment in the Face of Change by Diane G. Wilson

Do What You Are: Discover the Perfect Career for You Through the Secrets of Personality Type by Paul D. Tieger, Barbara Barron-Tieger

Do More Great Work. Stop The Busywork. Start The Work That Matters by Michael Bungay-Stanier

Do What You Love And The Money Will Follow by Marsha Sinetar

End Malaria by Michael Bungay Stanier

Frieda B. Herself by Renata Bowers

The Happiness Project by Gretchen Rubin

How Bad Do You Want It? (Achieve your needs, gain access to your wants with Network Marketing) by Candace Keefe and Elizabeth Vervynck

Life Makeovers: 52 Practical & Inspiring Ways to Improve Your Life One Week at a Time by Cheryl Richardson

The Millionaire Messenger by Brendon Burchard

The Missing Piece by Shel Silverstein*Monetize Your Passion* by Rich German

Oh, The Places You'll Go by Dr. Seuss

Second Careers by Caroline Bird

Secrets of Six-Figure Women: Surprising Strategies to Up Your Earnings and Change Your Life by Barbara Stanny

Think and Grow Rich by Napoleon Hill

Wishcraft by Barbara Sher

Websites to Enhance Your Journey:

http://www.abraham-hicks.com

http://www.art-is-fun.com

http://www.boxofcrayons.biz

http://www.friedab.com

http://www.napoleonhill.com

http://www.shaktigawain.com

http://www.ted.com

16423775R00064

Made in the USA
Charleston, SC
19 December 2012